How to Be Charlie One:
"Simply Being A Young Adult in an Adult World"

Bianca C. Brown

DEDICATION

This book is dedicated to the members of Charlie One and to all the confused young adults just trying to figure out life.

CONTENTS

Acknowledgments   i

1   Banking   Pg #4

2   How to buy a car and house   Pg #9

3   Insurance   Pg #19

4   Taxes   Pg #23

5   Government   Pg #26

ACKNOWLEDGMENTS

I just want to say thank you to all of my family and friends. Everyone has been above and beyond supportive since I launched my Kickstarter campaign for this book on Feb 24, 2017. Throughout this process, I have been overjoyed with how much care and support I have. I want to send special thanks to my contributors and people who believe in me and invested their time and money. I won't let you guys down.

I also want to thank my Imagination in Entrepreneurship teacher, Professor Tom Westbrook, at Oklahoma State University for pushing me. I hope I have 'amazed you. Seriously'.

INTRODUCTION

When I was overseas in Bahrain, my squad name was Charlie One. This group was the best group I have ever worked with. We came from all over the US; Oklahoma, Virginia, Ohio, Boston, Florida, Texas, and Utah. We each came together knowing something but we left knowing a little about everything. During my eleven months with Charlie One, I learned a lot about the home buying process and several other key things to life. At the end of deployment, I had gleaned a wealth of knowledge to which I brought back and applied to my young adult life. I learned how to save, invest, and think with my money.

When I finally settled back at home, I realized that many young adults have a lot of questions about adulthood. Like myself, I am sure many young adults have tried to "Google" or look up the ways of 'adulting' and failed. This is where my book comes in; how to simply be a young adult in an adult world. This is how to be Charlie One.

1 BANKING

In our world today when a person has a job they usually require direct deposit of some sort. I opened my first checking account with my mom when I was 16 years old. I felt great because I had $100. Seven years later, after paying bills, I hope and pray that I have a $100 left in my account. When I was overseas with Charlie One, I received several big checks every month. At the time, I would save a little and drink the rest. I learned that my other squad members were saving, investing and planning on making big ticket purchases when they returned home. Charlie One taught me how to save and invest on an adult level. I want to share my Charlie One knowledge with you.

For a young adult starting out in the adult world, it is good to have a bank account because it gives you security and helps you keep track of your finances. Having a bank account helps you avoid putting all your money in a proverbial mattress and then risking that mattress accidently catching on fire. When you have an account with the bank you have several options to include: checking account, savings account, or both. A checking account is meant for your daily spending and a savings account is meant to keep the money set aside (not spent) to gain interest. Most savings accounts have limited transactions each month as well. When you go to open your first bank account you need to know your social security number. You will also need a valid ID, your address, and yourself, that's the most important part.

In the realm of banking, there are multiple things a bank is useful for. Primarily, people go to the bank to get loans. The definition of loan *is an amount of money loaned at interest by a bank to a borrower, usually on collateral security, for a certain period of time.* In simple terms, a loan is borrowing money that will be paid back later with interest. Before we get too far ahead, interest is a percentage that is gained or charged on an amount of money loaned or saved. Bank loans, secured bank loans, and secured bank credit cards allow you to begin building a credit profile and/or credit score. Your credit score is this magical number that basically defines your financial life and whether creditors will lend to you on a future basis. It represents whether you are credit worthy i.e. loaning money on credit. The higher your credit score is the better! If you pay your bills on time, do not open up too many accounts within a two-year period, do not charge credit cards up to their maximum, pay off balances monthly, and/or pay more than just minimum limits on months you are unable to pay off your balance, then your credit score will increase. If you should file for bankruptcy, have a divorce, or experience large hospital bills then your credit score will decline significantly. Delinquent payments on your bills will lower your credit score as well "charge - off's" meaning accounts you default on resulting in the creditor reporting the debt as a failure to pay thereby charged-off as a loss on their books. Those debts are typically

5

purchased by debt collection companies whom will try to collect what they can from you. Most charged off accounts will typically fall off of your credit in approximately seven years. If you talk to a debt collection company, this renews the debt. After the initial charge-off, you may be able to dispute the amount with the three credit reporting agencies and the creditor will have to prove the debt was yours. If they are unable to, then the debt is removed from your credit report. Until such time, charge-off's have a significant negative effect on your credit score.

Back to loans, some major types of loans are personal loans, small business loans, car loans, home loans and commercial loans. Personal loans are used for private financial expenses. When taking out a loan, as a young adult make sure you look at the interest rate. Loan interest rates are based on your credit score. As a young adult, typically you have no credit or may stumbled into a bad credit situation unknowingly. Either way, you're screwed when it comes to interest rates. Why? Because the creditor is willing to give you a chance; however, should you default they at least made some sort of profit off of you before experiencing a forecasted default. Morale of the story, do not default! Ask for a refinance after six months of responsible pay history or attempt to renegotiate the rate.

If you are seeking to get a car loan, simply apply online. NOTE: Try to limit the amount of times apply for loans and look at your credit because it will start to lower your credit score. If you do it too much, it may signal the credit bureau's possible identity theft. While online, you will type in your personal information and any information about the vehicle should the require it. The bank will approve you for an amount based on your credit score. You will get a paper "approval letter" saying what you are allowed to spend and you can take that to the dealership and shop til' you drop.

At this age, you are begin getting a lot of mail from businesses pressuring you to sign up for credit cards. You have also probably heard a parent or 'real' adult say not to get a credit card ever in your life. Based on my research, there are pros and cons of a credit card:

- Pros:
  - You can increase your credit score
  - Credit cards are great for an emergency
  - When using a credit card correctly, you can earn cash back and rewards
- Cons
  - You can get into debit quickly
  - A short term credit card can hurt your credit score
  - Not making your payment will hurt your credit score even worse

As mentioned before, if you have a credit card, do not max out your limit. What I mean by that is if you are given a limit of $1,000; do not spend all $1,000. You have to pay all that money back plus interest meaning you might owe $1,500 in reality. Use your credit card for a portion of the limit and when you pay the bill make sure you pay more than the minimum balance at the very least.

WHERE MY COLLEGE PEOPLE AT?! I have been in college for four years now and in my fourth year. That said, I finally learned the difference between subsidized and unsubsidized loans. Super simple, subsidized loans **will** <u>not</u> gain interest while you are in school and unsubsidized loans **will gain** interest while you are in school. I wish somebody would have explained that to me in my freshman year.

Best tip about banking is to just call. Call a bank and ask questions. A lot of banks have rules and regulations that are different from one another. Many of the bank tellers are more than happy and understanding to answer your questions. Additionally, Bank Loan Officers are extremely useful in assisting you with getting started on your young adult financial journey. Happy Banking!

2 HOW TO BUY A CAR AND HOUSE

HOW TO BUY A CAR

As a driver, you should have a few thoughts of what you prefer to drive. If you are a sporty car guy or a crazy truck girl like me, then you generally know what you want. In our generation, you can do a lot of vehicle searching online before you even step foot onto an auto dealership. While on deployment, one of my teammates in Charlie One was looking to buy a new mustang when he returned home. This guy spent hours online looking at countless mustangs in his area. He was so ready he knew his credit score, his down payment, and his financing institution. In the United States, he had his best friend doing all of the footwork for him. When you go to buy your car here is some things to know.

Before you get to the dealership there are things that can help smooth out the car buying process. First, it helps to know what color and style of vehicle you prefer. You should know roughly what your credit score is and the price range you want. The dealership will automatically check your credit score too. Also, if you are buying a truck or SUV, know ahead of time if you want two wheel drive (2WD) or four wheel drive (4WD).

When I was buying my first truck, I really wanted a brand new lifted 2011 Dodge Ram Mega Cab. Unfortunately, at 16, I did not have lifted Dodge Ram Mega Cab type of money. I had to face reality of should I buy a used vehicle or a new vehicle. As a young adult that depends on you. (I ended up with a 1993 Chevy Silverado single cab.) So we will look at the pros and cons list:

- **Pros of having a new car**
    - They have warranties
- **Cons of having a new car**
    - It is expensive
    - As soon as you drive off the lot your vehicle depreciates by about $5,000

- **Pros of having a used car**
    - You do not have to worry about depreciating in value
    - Used cars are usually cheaper
- **Cons of having a used car**
    - The car already has miles on it
    - There may not be any warranties
    - The car might have previous mechanical problems

Let's stick to the idea you are interested in buying a used car and saving money. Every young adult likes to save money because we generally don't have any money.

8 things you should be aware of when buying a used car:

1. Be happy with your selection. You are going to be driving this car for hopefully 3 to 5 years.
2. Affordability. Make sure you select a vehicle you can afford. You will be making payments on this vehicle for 3 to 5 years.
3. Check the service history. You want to make sure your vehicle was taken care of by the previous owner because you will be servicing it for 3 to 5 years.
4. The year the car was made. The newer the car the better your interest rates will be and the better the reliability of the car. Try not to buy a car that is older than 5 years old because you will be driving it for the next 3 to 5 years too.
5. The warranties. You want to get a good warranty. You might have to use that warranty between the next 3 to 5 years.
6. Look at the interior and exterior. Make sure there is no extreme wear and tear damage. You will be driving this vehicle for the next 3 to 5 years so if somebody has beaten this car up before you it might not be too good.
7. Look under the hood. Check to see if anything is rigged, zip tied, duct taped or leaking. Young adults think duct tape fixes everything. Duct tape does fix everything except for the car that you will be driving for the next 3 to 5 years.
8. Low mileage. You should refrain from buying a car with high mileage. If you are buying a car with 50,000 miles or above the chance of having

problems are higher. Think about how many miles you will put on the vehicle while you own it for the next 3 to 5 years.

I hope from that list you understand that buying a car is a lengthy commitment. (yes, you guessed it, 3 to 5 years). The relationship with your car might be longer than relationships you have in your love life. Unlike a relationship with a human, you can take a car for a test drive. When you are test driving your car check for how it handles and how the engine feels. When you are accelerating or braking does the car make any odd noises or does the steering veer to a certain direction. If you are trying to drive straight and your car is driving to the left or to the right that means that car needs an alignment. After the test drive, visually check under the car for any leaks.

Imagine that you find a car that you like and a salesman approaches you. There are some red flags to a shady salesman such as:

- If you are at a dealership and the salesman says that he do not allow test drives; you should leave immediately.

- If your salesman is talking faster than you can text; you should leave immediately.

- If you ask your salesman specific questions and he doesn't directly answer your questions; you should leave immediately.

- If your salesman says something along the line of, "Oh, Yeah, we can take care of that," or "Sure, that's not a problem to fix." You should leave immediately.

- FOR ANY REASON, YOU HAVE THAT BUBBLE GUT FEELING OR BUTTERFLIES; YOU SHOULD LEAVE IMMEDIATELY!

Now, that I have steered you away from the sketchy car salesman, let's say you are at a more pleasurable dealership. A salesman should be attentive and willing to take their time and make sure you are comfortable and satisfied. If you tell the salesman that you do not have the full down payment for the vehicle, you can get a loan from the bank or just hustle, grind, and save for that down payment. The salesman can only help so much. As a young adult, a salesman might require you to have a co-signer. A co-signer is somebody who is willing to make the payments if you are unable to. If you miss a payment, your credit will be affected and so will your co-signers. Please do not screw over your co-signer, just make your payments.

You have now signed all the legal binding paperwork to your own vehicle. Congratulations! What's next? You need to get insurance. There is a small window to get insurance but get it immediately. Call the insurance company with all the vehicle information listed on your paperwork. Typically, an insurance company will ask for the year, make, model, and VIN number. The insurance company will also ask about your age and employment too. If you have taken a driver's education course, make sure you inform the agent as this typically will get you a discount by providing your certificate of completion. Lastly, depending on what state you live in, you will be mailed the title and lien of your vehicle within a few days. Some states will give you a paper tag that is usually good for 30 days until all your paperwork is mailed to you. Once you have the title, lien, valid driver's license and verification of insurance you can go to the tag agency and update the tags on your car. There is a cost for updating your tags. You can call your local tag agency and get an estimate.

Best tip about buying a car is to make your payments on time. Making your payments on time is the best way to not get your car repossessed. Enjoy your car but don't drive it into the ground. If you take care of your vehicle, your vehicle will take care of you. Repairs are expensive! Be mindful of your check engine light, it will not go away if you ignore it. If you ignore your check engine light long enough your engine will lock up and you'll just have to throw the whole car away and get a new one. Make sure you get your oil changed, new air filters, and tires rotated. On the positive side, after doing all this to buy a car it helps build your credit score.

HOW TO BUY A HOUSE

As a young adult, do not let your eyes get bigger than your pockets. Many GROWN adults already have established careers and tons of savings so they can afford their mini-mansion. As a young adult, WE HAVE NOTHING! When looking for a home, start small, look for something that you are able to live within your means. Unlike renting, when you own a home you pay for all of your expenses! You pay for your own lights, water, trash, cable, internet, lawn care, homeowner insurance, plus all of your other bills like your car payment, cell phone, gym membership, and of course school. Within Charlie One, several teammates owned homes. There was a guy from Boston who I would say was a real estate guru. At the time, he was investing towards having his basement redone. I wanted to buy a house when I came home but I did not know where the first step would be. I must say, my Charlie One real estate investment guy was a big key in my own 'how-to-buy-a-house-learning-process.'

First things first, when looking to buy a home you want to get "pre-approved." You contact a Loan Officer at a bank or at a private loan company. When you get connected with a Loan Officer, you will primarily discuss your salary and other expenses to determine your debt to income ratio thereby setting a limit on how much house you can afford. The process is kind of long and gets pretty deep into your financial life. After you have your pre-approval quote, you can start selecting a few houses to get serious about.

There is an outrageous amount of home loan options, a few to name are: the conventional home loan, the USDA home loan, FHA home loan and the VA home loan for the folks in the military. Your Loan Officer will help you figure out which home loan best suit your needs. With a home loan, you will be starting your mortgage origination process. A traditional loan is through the mortgage company and government loan requires you to get approved by the mortgage company plus the government also. There is not much of a difference from a traditional

15

mortgage loan and a government loan.

When buying a house, a good down payment is usually 10% to 20%. The dictionary defines a mortgage as *a conveyance of an interest in property as security for the repayment of money borrowed.* A mortgage in simple terms is money you owe for property you buy. A better way to think of a mortgage is instead of paying rent to somebody else, you are paying a mortgage to your own house.

When you find a house you really like you will need to have that home inspected. Customarily, home inspections are done by the mortgage company. The mortgage company regularly has a list of home inspectors that they rotate to call. In some states, the Buyer is required to find their own Inspector too.

Once you get this far in your home buying process, your Realtor should definitely help with many questions. As you are finishing up the process one of the last steps is closing cost. The definition of closing cost is *any expenses over the purchase price of a house, land, etc., that is paid by the purchaser or seller at the completion of the sale.* Essentially, closing cost is the cost of putting together all the paperwork, filing the paperwork and the cost of inspections. The closing cost covers anything that is outside of the mortgage. Your closing cost will depend on the price of the house. The higher the cost of the house, the higher the closing cost will be.

There are some classes or programs that can help reduce the cost for you. Programs organized with government loans will pay your down payment up to 5%. The main qualification is you have to make under a certain amount of money plus a few other things too. A few mortgage companies will offer their own classes to help with more things you need to know. Additionally, your Realtor can negotiate with the Seller's Realtor to pay a portion of your closing costs, and/or you can have a slighter higher rate in order to obtain a Lender's credit towards closing costs.

Hypothetically, you find the lovely starter house you always pictured yourself in. Once you are moved in don't forget about property taxes and home insurance! Property tax is largely a tax based on what the county feels like your property is worth and you give that money to the government each year. Home insurance is insurance that covers your house in case of disaster or a variety of unfortunate events to include "acts of God" such as a tornado. If you do not have home insurance, you are 100% responsible for fixing anything on your house. Lenders typically will require that their investment i.e. your investment has homeowners insurance in place. Additionally, taxes and insurance can be escrowed. An escrow is a type of savings account with the Lender whereby they collect the monthly amount (12/taxes and 12/HOI) and place this into said account until time as these bills are due. Instead you paying the large bill, the Lender sends a check each year at the time of renewal and/or payment.

As a new buyer, 5 things you should be looking for when purchasing a home:

- Location
- Price

- School District
- Community
- Curb Appeal

You might have your own personal wants and needs for your home too. When buying a home, don't forget that you are making an investment. Many young adults don't think about a house being a future investment and they miss the thought of reselling in the future. NOTE: Do not buy a two bedroom house unless you have really good plans of renting it out. A two bedroom house has an extremely difficult resale value/potential.

Best tip for the home buying process is you should be working with a Realtor. Your Realtor should be professional and easy to work with. You should feel comfortable with your Realtor as they are helping you make a big decision. A Realtor should be very detailed about everything for you. They should make sure you have full understanding of the whole process. Make sure you are ready to own a home. You will be owning your home a lot longer than your car and maybe a little longer than some relationships too.

3 INSURANCE

First things first, Charlie One had insurance during the deployment. Charlie One was a fun, pranking, and adventurous group of people; there were several times things could have gone bad. Before and after deployment, Charlie One sat through approximately ten hours of insurance power points. I am sure you know that power points are boring so just imagine our pain and suffering. Yes, cerebral death by power point is a serious affliction. Personally, I still couldn't tell you much about my insurance even after said ten hours of death by power point. We know that insurance is that thing or card that everybody needs when they drive a car and when they go to the hospital but really what is insurance and how does it work?

The definition of insurance is *the act, system, or business of insuring property, life, one's person, etc., against loss or harm arising in specified contingencies, as fire, accident, death, disablement, or the like, in consideration of a payment proportionate to the risk involved.*

In the simplest terms, insurance is the act of transferring risk. You pay a company to pay your claims. You take a small amount of the risk and the insurance company takes on the big risk.

The main types of insurance a young adult should consider having is:

- Renters insurance
- Auto insurance
- Life insurance
- Health insurance
- Homeowner insurance

Renters insurance can be wonderful for a young adult like you because you probably live in an apartment. Normally, renters insurance covers your stuff and other people's stuff. Perhaps, that your mattress with all the cash; the cash that you should have put in the bank, it catches fire and burns down the apartment complex. With renters insurance everybody is covered. Renters insurance can be as cheap as $20 a month and cover about $20,000. You can increase the amount if you deem necessary. Personally, I don't have $20,000 worth of stuff in my house. The most expensive thing I own is my PlayStation and my TV.

Auto insurance comes in basically 3 different types. There is comprehensive car insurance which covers the vehicle for things that are out of your control like theft, fire, or hail. There is collision coverage which covers things that are your fault such as you hit another vehicle or slide on black ice and run over a sweet little old lady's mailbox. Lastly, is liability coverage which pays for the other person's, medical bills and property damage. Each insurance agency might call these types of coverage different names but the gist of the coverage should be the same.

You are probably having the same thought as I did, which was, why do I need life insurance? For example, if you buy a life insurance plan when you are 23 years old then hypothetically payments will only be approximately $10 a month. On the other hand, if you try to purchase a life insurance plan when you are partially cripple, been diagnosed with diabetes, high blood pressure, and have had 3 knee surgeries than your payments will be like $120 a month. You are more of a liability to die when you are older than when you are younger. For the most part, do not purchase life insurance just thinking it's to cover the funeral cost. The money from the insurance is to be used as a substantial check to pay off remaining bills and other expenses that you left behind for your loved ones to contend with.

A common term in the insurance realm is the word 'deductible.' The definition for deductible *is the amount for which the insured is liable on each loss, injury, etc., before an insurance company will make payment.* In simple terms, a deductible is the amount of money you pay up front while the insurance covers the rest. For example, if there was $5,000 worth of damages and you have a $1,000 deductible then you will pay $1,000 and your insurance company will send you a check for $4,000. The same scenario works for health insurance also.

Health insurance is very similar to the other insurances. Instead of having a deductible you have what is called co-pay. Co-pay works the same way as a deductible does as far as you pay a certain amount and the insurance company will cover the rest. To find the best health insurance, it is best to comparison shop different company rates via website and/or a phone call.

Best tip about insurance is to get what you need. If you think you can afford to have renters insurance, life insurance, and health insurance then get some. It is better to be safe than sorry. Of course, if you are driving you must have auto insurance.

4 TAXES

From being with Charlie One, I learned that if you have kids you get a bigger tax return! On the bad side, if you have kids, you have to pay for them all year long too. I still do not have any children and pets do not count unfortunately unless you own a farm. The military, along with every other job in America, has taxes taken out of your check. Until I was with Charlie One, I never gave much attention to the withholding boxes on my check stubs. Charlie One taught me that the withholding amounts on your stubs make a big difference in how your taxes are paid.

By now we all know that everybody needs to pay taxes. To begin, your taxes you would need your W2 form from your job. A W2 is basically an annual statement an employer provides to you of what you earned and what was withheld from federal, medical and social security. Most people obtain their W2 after January 31st annually. State taxes and federal taxes are very similar. The state tax is anticipation of what your tax liability is for the year and federal is the same anticipation but for the federal government.

When you file your taxes you will need a few documents. Commonly, you need your W2 from any job you worked within the year. You will also need your social security card if you do not know your own social from memory and an ID card. If you are a college student, you should receive a 1098-T from your school which notes the cost of tuition and amount of scholarships and grants. The easiest way to do your taxes is by yourself if you re single. There are plenty 'do-it-yourself' software such as TurboTax available. If you are married or have children then you should use a tax service to help prepare you're taxes. You can call a tax company and ask them how much their rates are ahead of time. Once your taxes are completed, it usually takes about 2 to 3 weeks for you to receive your money via direct deposit.

TAXES CAN GET UGLY

If you don't pay your taxes or file your taxes the government has special ways to haunt your life. Some reasons young adults owe on their taxes is because they aren't withholding enough from the state or federal sections. If you do not withhold any money from your checks at tax time you will end up owing money. Your tax money can get garnished if you have unpaid child support and unpaid student loans, and/or a few other special situations. If you do not file your taxes you are only hurting yourself. For example, you file your taxes in 2010. In 2011, 2012, 2013, and 2014 you did not file your taxes. In 2015, you realize you want to get your life right and you file your taxes. You would have to find your W2's and other necessary paperwork for the years of 2011-2014. If you were supposed to get a refund in 2011 or 2012 you can no longer receive that refund because you can only hold a check for 3 years. Or say you owe the government money; you will have to pay for all the years you missed. NOTE: if you need to raise your withholding amount on your checks, simply contact your human resource or payroll department.

4 tips for a young adult about their taxes:

- Keep a current address. Taxes get really messy when you change your address every 2 months.
- Keep track of where you work and your W2's. If you change multiple jobs and multiple addresses the companies you worked for lose track of where to send your W2's to.
- Don't make any of your tax decisions based on what your friend told you. Do not believe your friend when they say they got a refund of $10,000 by going to the shady tax guy at the end of the street. You know for a fact your friend didn't work all year long. Don't believe them, it's a trap.
- Check with your parents to see if they claimed you on their tax returns as a dependent or if you should file your taxes by yourself.

5 GOVERNMENT

Most of us sat through a government or civics class in high school but what did we really learn? From my experience, I understood the big picture such as congress, Supreme Court, the legislative, executive, and judicial branches. What I did not quite remember was the local government section. Now that I am out of high school adults always say, "Go vote in your local elections! It will help make the community better." Well, as much as I would love to vote in my local election, I do not know the first step to take. Charlie One did not talk much about politics or government but we all agreed that everybody should register to vote. With all of Charlie One being from different states there was not much conversation on local government either but what is the most adult-like thing to do? Go vote in your local elections.

Local government is different upon where you live. I live in Stillwater, Oklahoma and we have a committee made up of a mayor and several city councilors. They are the governing body of the city. City Council meetings are open to the public by law. Usually, an agenda is published prior to each meeting and is available at the meeting too. Nowadays most cities have their meeting on TV which is usually the boring channel that we skip to get to ESPN.

When it comes to registering to vote it becomes slightly tricky. Registering to vote is a single process. Depending on where you live there are a few determining factors. Perhaps you register as a republican then you are a republican for local and presidential elections. If there was a local election and there were no republications running then you could not vote in that election. Where you live determines where you vote. If there was an issue that became addressed in a meeting that was concerning a certain area and you do not live in that area you do not get to vote on that issue. If you move, you need to change your registration address too. If you move out of a district, your voting location will change too.

You can change your party affiliation whenever you want. I'm talking about political parties not beer drinking parties. If you want to belong to a certain party then you can, if you don't, you can be registered as an Independent voter. Sometimes people register as a certain party even though they do not agree with all the political party ideas.

When you do go to vote on an issue or for an election the places are called polling places. Most polling places are spread out all over town and are often in churches or schools. Very rarely occasions the polling place is held at a residence.

I always thought when I get older, I would supernaturally know more about politics. My supernatural political powers never came. I had to go figure out politics on my own. If you want to know more about the issues and topics being discussed the information is much easier to find than what you think. You could watch local government TV prior to the elections, read the local newspaper, or get a printed agenda of the council meetings from your municipal buildings. Many cities have question and answer forums held by special political groups. For the best information resources, attend local government meetings or just read the newspaper. The newspaper has a government section.

Before writing this book, I always wanted to know was local voting anything like presidential voting. Come to find out, local voting is exactly like voting for the president. Same procedure. Same Locations. Same type of ballots. Same 'I Voted' stickers. Congratulations. Civic responsibility, duty, and privilege accomplished!

If you now feel comfortable voting in the next presidential election this is how you go about doing so. I wanted to vote in 2012 but I honestly had no clue where to go register or what to bring. To register for the presidential election you can go to several places. You can always call the election board or your city hall to give directions on where your local places are. When you go to the polling place to vote, you should bring your voter ID card and your driver's licenses or a state ID.

Perhaps, you are like I used to be and you are not interested in politics at all. In all honesty, very few people actually care about all political issues but probably everyone cares about some issues. Since you are getting older, take the time to read about some issues and some candidates. If you are really don't care about political whatsoever – then don't complain when things change. If you give your best effort to trying to understand politics than you are the best type of person there is. Politics are meant to be somewhat complicated.

5 easy things to do to be more educated about local government

- Read the local paper.
- Read local government meeting agendas.
- Watch the local TV stations when they interview local politicians like the mayor.
- Go to the city meetings. You can ask as many questions as you want, everybody will be thrilled.
- Listen to NPR. (National Public Radio)

CLOSING WORDS FROM THE AUTHOR

Deployment with Charlie One literally changed my life. I would have not asked for a different squad to serve with overseas. I did not learn one lesson but an extraordinary amount of insight to work with. It takes a motivated and determined person to take what they learned and apply it to their life. Shame on the people who withhold knowledge for themselves. The people of Charlie One probably didn't know that a year later they would be a part of a book concept but they really inspired me to get my life going. I hope by reading "How to be Charlie One" you learned 'how to be a young adult in an adult world.' This book was not written to give all the answers but to put you on the right path to take your first step with mature decisions. With all the knowledge that you have read in this book, GO! Take your first big steps of life and share "How to be Charlie One"!

Charlie One - Bahrain 2016

REFERENCES

If you live in or near the area of Stillwater, Oklahoma and you have further questions about the chapters discussed these people are more than willing to chat with you and answer any questions that you may have.

IBC Bank
(405) 372-0889

Stillwater Tax Service
Ricky Lawson
(405) 377-6113
Stwtaxservice15@gmail.com

Insurance
Marcie Atkinson
Marcie-atkinson@yahoo.com

Special thanks to Dictionary.com for technical definitions.

www.ingramcontent.com/pod-product-compliance
Lightning Source LLC
Chambersburg PA
CBHW060502210326
41520CB00015B/4055